GRILL
IT
UP

FLAVORFUL &
FUN RECIPES
FOR THE BBQ

STEVE
TILLETT

GIBBS SMITH
TO ENRICH AND INSPIRE HUMANKIND

First Edition
22 21 20 19 18   5 4 3 2 1

Published by
Gibbs Smith
P.O. Box 667
Layton, Utah 84041

1.800.835.4993 orders
www.gibbs-smith.com

Designed by Rita Sowins
Food styling by Marcela Ferrinha and Corrine Miller
Printed and bound in Hong Kong
Gibbs Smith books are printed on either recycled, 100% post-consumer waste,
FSC-certified papers or on paper produced from sustainable PEFC-certified forest/
controlled wood source. Learn more at www.pefc.org.

Library of Congress Cataloging-in-Publication Data

Names: Tillett, Steve, author.
Title: Grill it up : flavorful & fun recipes for the BBQ / Steve Tillett.
Description: First edition. | Layton, Utah : Gibbs Smith, 2018.
Identifiers: LCCN 2017036334 | ISBN 9781423648536 (hardcover)
Subjects: LCSH: Barbecuing. | LCGFT: Cookbooks.
Classification: LCC TX840.B3 .T556 2018 | DDC 641.7/6--dc23
LC record available at https://lccn.loc.gov/2017036334

This book is dedicated to my father who was the paragon of "How to Win Friends and Influence People." Mr. Carnegie must have written about you. I love you dad.

To my amazing wife Sharon—we planted our garden together nearly 30 years ago. We have toiled to keep it fertilized, watered, and flourishing. In spite of my many flaws, she has stayed by my side and, at times, dragged me along. Weeds have crept in, but with quick attention we have evicted those weeds together before they could choke out the fruits of our labors. I am excited for the years to come and to enjoy the continued fruits of our harvest. There is no work I am not willing to do to keep her close by my side as we enjoy the life we have built together.

CONTENTS

HELPFUL HINTS

Grilling "low and slow" is the often-heard adage and barbecue mantra. If you say "cook it low and slow" to a grill enthusiast, their response, usually accompanied by a grin, is, "Yep, low and slow."

The goal with grilling low and slow is to avoid the intense heat that dries the meat out; the outside becomes too well-done and the juices are lost along with their flavor. Ideally, you can set up the grill to cook via indirect heat. This can be done by using a second, or a top shelf, turning off part of the gas grill to create a cooler area, or even covering part of the grate with heavy-duty aluminum foil.

No matter how you do it, the concept is the same; you are modifying the cooking area to be more indirect, such as an oven. The advantages of this method will help the meat you are grilling remain moist and flavorful, and you typically don't need to turn the meat as often. The meat cooks more evenly throughout, and you avoid the charring or burning caused from direct flames.

Still, is there an appropriate time to grill "hot and fast?" Here is the long-of-the-short, or the short-of-the-long, answer my father "Big Red" Ron Tillett, the butcher, used to give. "Crank the heat for the thinner cut of meat. For a thicker cut, take a seat on your butt."

1. The internal temperature of a cooked cut of meat not only defines safe cooking, but determines how tender, juicy, and flavorful it will be. The best way to improve your grilling skills is to invest in a good digital instant-read meat thermometer. This will take the guess work out of trying to determine if the meat is done to your liking, or cooked to a recommended safe temperature to help avoid foodborne illness.

2. It is best to baste the barbecue sauce on when the meat is done cooking. If you apply barbecue sauce to your meat before it is done, it will most assuredly burn. You're not trying to cook the sauce. However, a nice trick is to heat the sauce prior to applying it to the meat. Once you apply the sauce, it takes no more than a minute or two to get the sauce to set up (glazed over) and hold onto the skin.

3. Turn meat with tongs, instead of a fork, so you limit the loss of natural juices from puncturing the meat.

4. Boil leftover marinade in a saucepan over high heat. This kills any bacteria left by raw meat and makes it safe to use for basting during the last 5 minutes of grilling, or as a warm sauce for the finished dish.

5. Liquid smoke used in small amounts is a great way to make your food taste like it spent all day in the smoker.

6. Smoking foods on a gas grill is easy. The only things needed are wood chips and a smoker box. Pick up smoker wood chips from a local sporting goods store. Apple, cherry, hickory, or mesquite chips work well for pork, beef, or poultry. Try alder for fish.

7. If you don't own a smoker box or don't want to buy one, smoker pouches are easy to make. Follow these simple instructions:

   Use a large piece of heavy-duty aluminum foil, about 12 inches long. Place wood chips in the middle and wrap securely. Poke holes in top of pouch with a meat thermometer and it's ready to go. For large cuts of meat such as roasts, place the wood chips in water and soak for 30 minutes to 2 hours then place wood chips in smoker pouch. For smaller cuts of meat, dry chips are fine.

   Place your smoker pouch under the grilling grate, directly over the flame. Turn grill to high heat until smoke begins to rise from the pouch. Immediately turn grill down to desired cooking temperature and cook your food at the appropriate temperature, letting the wood chips go to work.

8. Meat becomes more tender when cooked slowly at a low temperature, no matter how high the grade. Also, meat served hot is usually more tender than meat served cold.

9. As a general rule, use approximately 1 $\frac{1}{2}$ cups of marinade for every 1 to 2 pounds of meat. Make sure it completely covers the meat. Let your meat marinate in a large ziplock bag in the refrigerator. Double bag to prevent leaks. You can also freeze marinating meats for future uses.

10. Marinade is the quickest way to tenderize meat and add additional zest. A quick 30-minute marinate will give meat a great taste. Marinating even longer will give you more flavor. When marinating in the refrigerator, remove meat and let it come to room temperature before grilling.

11. To help prevent your food from sticking, spray the grill grate with cooking spray, or wipe with oil prior to grilling. This will also make it easier to clean the grill once you're done.

12. To clean the grill after using, lay a piece of aluminum foil over the grate, shiny side down, and turn to high heat for 5 minutes. This will burn off any buildup on the grates. Watch the grill closely and do not leave unattended. When the 5 minutes are up, gently brush the grate with a wire brush.

13. For a grill that needs some serious cleaning, try using 2 tablespoons of baking soda added to 1 cup water. Brush it on with your wire brush, let sit for 2–3 minutes, and then scrub with the wire brush.

ADVANCED GRILLING TIPS

BEEF

Cook beef according to taste for the amount of time shown below.

Thickness	Doneness	Grilling Time Per Side
1 inch	rare	3–4 minutes
	medium	5–7 minutes
1½ inches	rare	5–7 minutes
	medium	8–9 minutes
2 inches	rare	7–9 minutes
	medium	9–11 minutes

Cook roast according to taste for the amount of time and temperature shown below.

Rare	140 degrees	20 minutes per pound
Medium	160 degrees	25 minutes per pound
Well	170 degrees	30 minutes per pound

To barbecue, turn grill to high heat, approximately 450 degrees F. The hotter the grill, the better it will seal in the juices. Place beef on grate and sear 30–60 seconds on each side, using tongs to turn so the natural juices stay sealed. Turn grill down to medium and finish cooking according to taste and desired doneness. Turn meat several times throughout total grilling time.

POULTRY

The trick to grilling chicken is to do it slowly and turn it frequently. Approximate cooking time is 20–30 minutes for chicken breasts, tenders, or thighs, and 20 minutes per pound if chicken is whole.

When cooking chicken with skin on, put a layer of heavy-duty aluminum foil on the bottom grate of the grill and cook the chicken on the middle or top rack. This will reduce the flare-ups and decrease the chance of burning.

To check if chicken is cooked through, squeeze it. When the juices run clear it is probably done. Double-check by using an instant-read thermometer placed into the thickest portion of the meat, making sure not to touch any bone. The temperature should be 165 degrees F.

To thaw frozen chicken, remove from freezer and place in the refrigerator the day before use. If in a hurry or for same-day use, place chicken in a bowl and fill with cool water. Allow to soak until thawed. Change water every few minutes to speed up the process.

PORK

The guidelines for safely preparing pork have changed, and now recommend pork to be cooked to an internal temperature of 145 degrees F, followed by a 5 minute rest time.

Pork is naturally drier than other meats. Do not to overcook it. Approximate cooking time is 30–35 minutes per pound. Using an instant-read thermometer will alleviate the guess work.

Marinades and brines will add a lot of flavor while helping to moisten your pork.

SEAFOOD

When grilling fish, do not turn it, and quickly remove it from grill when it is no longer opaque. Do not overcook.

Rubbing the grate with oil will help keep the fish from sticking.

Leave scales on bigger fish and cook scale side down. Salmon on the grill is best cooked on top of aluminum foil.

Grill trout over low but direct heat to add a hearty smoked flavor.

Other fish, like swordfish, tuna, mackerel, and bluefish, are great choices for grilling because their natural oils help keep them moist and flaky.

Thicker fillets stand up to the heat of the grill better than thin ones.

Using a grill basket or aluminum foil for thinner fillets of fish can keep it from falling apart.

GRILL YOUR
GREENS

PARMESAN POTATO WEDGES

MAKES 4 TO 6 SERVINGS

4 medium potatoes, cut lengthwise into ¼-inch-thick wedges

2 tablespoons olive oil

4 tablespoons freshly grated Parmesan cheese

Salt and freshly ground pepper or favorite seasoning salt, to taste

Ranch dressing or dipping sauce, of choice

Preheat grill to medium.

Place potato wedges in a large ziplock bag, add oil, cheese, and salt and pepper. Seal the bag and gently toss to coat potatoes.

Remove potatoes from the bag and place in a grill basket, or lay directly on the grill across the grates so they won't fall through. Grill, turning every 3–4 minutes, until desired tenderness. Remove from grill and serve warm with a side of ranch dressing or favorite dipping sauce.

GRILLED ASPARAGUS

MAKES 4 SERVINGS

1 pound thick asparagus spears

1 to 2 tablespoons olive oil

Salt and freshly ground pepper, Steve's Famous Dry Rub (page 125), or garlic salt, to taste

Preheat grill to medium high.

Remove the woody ends of the asparagus, by cutting with a knife or bending stalks until they snap, leaving the greener, tender portions of the stalk. Rinse well with water and pat dry with paper towels.

Place asparagus in a large ziplock bag, add oil and seasoning of choice, and gently massage bag to evenly coat asparagus. Remove from bag and lay the asparagus spears crosswise on grill so they won't fall through the grate, or place in a grill basket. Grill, turning every 2–3 minutes, to desired tenderness.

GRILLED SUMMER VEGGIES

MAKES 3 TO 5 SERVINGS

1 medium zucchini

1 large red bell pepper

1 pound fresh asparagus

1 pound cherry tomatoes

1/4 cup olive oil, plus more if needed

Salt and freshly ground pepper, favorite seasoning salt, or Steve's Famous Dry Rub (page 125), to taste.

Preheat grill to medium low.

Wash the vegetables and pat dry with paper towels. Cut the zucchini and bell pepper into 1/2-inch-thick slices or wedges. Cut the woody ends off of the asparagus and leave the tomatoes whole.

Place vegetables in a large bowl and drizzle oil sparingly over top. Add the seasoning and toss gently to coat. Place vegetables in a grill basket* and place basket on the grill. Cook, turning every 3–4 minutes, until done to your liking.

These grilled vegetables are great served hot off the grill with a side of ranch dressing, or chilled and served as a cold side or in place of a green salad.

*Tip: If you don't have a grill basket, fold a long piece of heavy-duty aluminum foil in half and fold up the edges to create a tray.

GARLIC BAKED POTATOES

MAKES 6 SERVINGS

6 large russet potatoes

6 tablespoons butter, softened

Garlic salt, to taste

SUGGESTED TOPPINGS

Butter, sour cream, salt and pepper, chopped green onions, grated cheese, bacon crumbles, ranch dressing, salsa, or grilled vegetables

Preheat grill to medium high.

Scrub the potatoes and then poke several times with a fork. Completely cover each potato with a thin coating of butter and sprinkle evenly with garlic salt.

Place potatoes on grill grate out of direct heat. Close lid and bake 40–50 minutes, or until potatoes are tender when pierced, turning a couple of times during cooking. Serve with favorite toppings.

MIX-AND-MATCH VEGGIE KEBABS

MAKES 4 TO 6 SERVINGS

2 small zucchini

2 small yellow squash

1 to 2 yellow bell peppers

1 to 2 red bell peppers

1 sweet onion, such as Walla-Walla or Vidalia

1 to 2 carrots*

10 to 20 cherry tomatoes

10 to 20 fresh cremini mushrooms

1/4 cup olive oil, plus more if needed

Salt and freshly ground pepper, Steve's Famous Dry Rub (page 125), or garlic salt, to taste

6 (10- to 12-inch) metal or bamboo* skewers

Preheat grill to medium.

Cut all of the vegetables except tomatoes and mushrooms into 1/2-inch-thick slices or wedges. Place vegetables in a large ziplock bag, add oil and seasoning of choice, and gently toss to evenly coat.

Thread vegetable pieces onto the skewers,* making sure to place the more solid vegetables on both ends so that the softer vegetables don't fall off. Lay the skewers on the grill at a 90 degree angle across the grates and turn every 3–4 minutes until you reach the desired tenderness, about 10–15 minutes.

*Tips: If you are using carrots or new potatoes, try boiling them for a few minutes until barely softened so they will slide a little more easily onto the skewer.

If you use wooden or bamboo skewers, soak them in water for 30 minutes prior to using so they don't burn.

Add flavor by brushing the veggies with an infused oil.

GARLIC-INFUSED OLIVE OIL

1 to 2 tablespoons minced fresh garlic

1/2 cup olive oil

1 1/2 teaspoons dried oregano or herb of choice, optional

Place garlic, oil, and oregano in a small saucepan. Gently warm the oil over medium-low heat, stirring often, until the garlic starts to turn golden brown. Remove from heat and transfer to a bowl to cool. When cooled, place in an airtight container and store in refrigerator for up to 1 month.

CORN ON THE COB

MAKES 6 SERVINGS

6 ears corn in their husks

1 stick butter, softened

Salt and freshly ground pepper, to taste

Preheat grill to medium high.

Cut off the corn silk at ends of husks and discard. Place corn on rack, close the lid and cook, turning frequently for 15–20 minutes, or until kernels are tender when pierced. Remove from grill.

When cool enough to handle, remove husks and any remaining corn silk. Serve with butter, and salt and pepper.

Variation: Brush a light coat of mayonnaise over cooked corn and sprinkle with freshly grated Parmesan cheese.

SPICY ITALIAN VEGGIES

MAKES 3 TO 5 SERVINGS

4 Roma tomatoes

1 large red onion

2 medium yellow squash

2 green bell peppers

¼ cup Italian salad dressing, or to taste

2 teaspoons dried basil

Salt and freshly ground pepper, to taste

Preheat grill to medium high.

Cut the vegetables into ½-inch-thick slices or wedges. Place in a large bowl and add the dressing, tossing gently to coat. Place coated vegetable pieces in a grill basket, peel side down, and sprinkle with basil and salt and pepper. Grill 4–6 minutes, or until heated through. Do not turn.

Variation: For an even spicier version, marinate vegetables in dressing for up to 6 hours.

BUTTER AND GARLIC VEGETABLES

MAKES 6 TO 8 SERVINGS

2 medium zucchini

1 medium yellow squash

3 pattypan squash

2 red bell peppers

1 pound fresh asparagus

1 pound fresh mushrooms

4 tablespoons melted butter

1 teaspoon minced garlic

Seasoning salt or salt and freshly ground pepper, to taste

Preheat grill to medium high.

Cut all the vegetables, except asparagus and mushrooms, into $\frac{1}{4}$- to $\frac{1}{2}$-inch-thick slices or wedges and place in a large bowl.

In a small bowl, mix together the butter and garlic then pour over the vegetables and toss to coat. Place vegetables in a grill basket and cook until tender, 5–10 minutes, depending on the thickness of the vegetables, and turning every 1–2 minutes. Check individual vegetables for tenderness and remove from heat to a serving dish when cooked as desired. Sprinkle with seasoning salt, or salt and pepper, and serve.

CABBAGE ON THE GRILL

MAKES 6 SERVINGS

1 large head cabbage

Butter, to taste

2 teaspoons onion powder or salt

Salt and freshly ground pepper, to taste

Preheat grill to medium and lightly oil grate.

Cut cabbage into 4 to 8 wedges and remove core. Place wedges on a piece of heavy-duty aluminum foil large enough to wrap and completely cover cabbage. Dot wedges with pats of butter, sprinkle with onion powder, season with salt and pepper, and seal foil tightly; place directly on grill grate. Grill for 30 minutes, or until tender.

GRILLED SQUASH AND ONIONS

MAKES 3 TO 5 SERVINGS

2 to 3 small zucchini

2 to 3 small yellow squash

2 small purple onions, peeled

¼ cup olive oil, plus more if needed

2 teaspoons garlic powder

1 teaspoon lemon juice

Salt and freshly ground pepper, to taste

Preheat grill to medium high.

Cut the vegetables into ¼- to ½-inch-thick slices or wedges. In a small bowl, combine the oil, garlic powder, and lemon juice; mix well. Place vegetables in a large bowl, pour mixture over top, and toss to coat.

Turn the grill down to medium low and place vegetables in a grill basket. Place on the grill grate and cook for 4–6 minutes, or until tender, turning every minute or so. Sprinkle with salt and pepper.

GRILLED ACORN SQUASH

MAKES 2 TO 4 SERVINGS

2 acorn squash

Butter, to taste

Salt and pepper, to taste

Preheat grill to medium.

Wrap each squash individually in heavy-duty aluminum foil with a pat of butter. Place on grill grate, close lid, and cook for 20–30 minutes, or until tender.

Remove from grill and slice squash in half lengthwise; scoop out any seeds and strings.

Place the halves back on the grill, cut side up. Add another 2 to 3 pats of butter directly on top of the squash and let cook for 5–10 more minutes, or until butter is mostly absorbed.

Remove from grill, season with salt and pepper and serve.

Variation: Slice each of the squash halves into 1-inch wedges and place back on the grill until light grill marks appear.

ON THE LIGHTER SIDE

PIZZA BITES

MAKES 2 PIZZAS

Olive oil, for grill grate

2 (12-inch) premade pizza crusts

1 tablespoon extra virgin olive oil, divided

2 cups crushed tomatoes or favorite pizza sauce, divided

2 to 3 cups freshly grated mozzarella, divided

Pizza toppings such as: pepperoni, prosciutto, salami, Canadian bacon, cooked sausage, cooked bacon crumbles, olives, tomato slices, fresh mushrooms, artichoke hearts, roasted red or yellow bell peppers, or sliced green onions

¼ cup minced fresh rosemary, fresh basil leaves, torn into small pieces, or fresh oregano leaves, divided, optional

Freshly grated Parmesan cheese, optional

Preheat grill to medium high.

Using tongs, dip a folded paper towel in olive oil* and rub over the grill grates.

Brush the top of each pizza crust lightly with ½ tablespoon olive oil and spread 1 cup of crushed tomatoes or pizza sauce evenly over the top to within ½ inch of the edge. Sprinkle about 1 to 1 ½ cups of mozzarella over the sauce and add 2 to 3 of your favorite toppings (you don't want to overload the pizza).

Carefully slide pizzas onto the grill grates out of direct heat, close the lid, and cook for 5–10 minutes, or until the cheese melts, checking often to make sure the bottom doesn't burn. If the bottom is getting too dark, but the toppings still need more time to heat or melt, lower the heat, place the pizzas on a couple of pieces of heavy-duty aluminum foil or a pizza stone, close the lid, and continue to cook, checking every 2 minutes. When cooked to liking, remove pizzas from the grill and transfer to a cutting board. Sprinkle tops with fresh herbs and Parmesan cheese. Cut into small wedges or squares and serve with a side salad for a light lunch.

Variation: Use pita bread, naan, flatbread, French bread, or garlic bread.

*Tips: To enhance the flavor of the pizza crust, brush the grill grates with Garlic-Infused Olive Oil (page 21).

To avoid burning or overcooking the crust, place a pizza stone on grill grate and cook the pizza on the stone for about 10–12 minutes, or until cheese is melted and starts to bubble.

GRILLED GARLIC BREAD

1 loaf French or Italian bread

4 tablespoons butter, softened

1 to 2 tablespoons minced fresh garlic or garlic salt, or to taste

½ cup freshly grated Parmesan cheese

Preheat grill to low.

Cut bread in half lengthwise. Place cut side down on grill and lightly toast. Remove bread from grill and set aside. In a small bowl, mix together the butter, garlic, and Parmesan cheese until well-combined. Spread mixture on toasted side of bread. Place bread back on the grill out of direct heat, buttered side up. Close the lid and cook until the cheese mixture is hot and melted.

HOMEMADE CROUTONS

MAKES 6 TO 8 SERVINGS

1 loaf day-old French bread

½ cup olive or vegetable oil

1 to 2 tablespoons garlic powder, or to taste

2 tablespoons dried sweet basil

Preheat grill to medium.

Cut bread into 1-inch cubes and place in a large bowl. Drizzle oil over bread cubes until lightly covered and sprinkle with garlic powder and basil; toss to coat.

Place coated bread cubes in a grill basket in a single layer, place on grill, and cook for 10–15 minutes, or until toasted to a light golden brown; turn frequently.

GREEK PASTRY PIZZA

MAKES 4 TO 6 SERVINGS

¼ cup olive oil

¼ teaspoon salt

2 to 4 teaspoons minced fresh garlic, or to taste

1 loaf French, ciabatta, or focaccia bread

TOPPINGS

1 cup grated mozzarella cheese

2 Roma tomatoes, sliced

¼ to ½ cup artichoke hearts

¼ cup black or Kalamata olives, halved

2 green onions, sliced

2 ounces crumbled feta cheese

2 tablespoons chopped fresh basil

Preheat grill to medium high.

Combine oil, salt, and garlic together in a small bowl. Cut the bread in half and then cut each half lengthwise. Brush garlic mixture evenly over the cut side of each piece of bread. Carefully place bread halves cut side down on the grill and toast for 1–2 minutes, or until it begins to brown. Remove from grill.

Divide topping ingredients evenly and layer over the toasted side of each piece of bread in order listed. Return the prepared bread to the grill, close lid, and continue to cook for 2–4 minutes, or until the bottom starts to brown and the cheese has melted. If cheese is slow to melt, move the bread to upper rack of the grill and close the lid. Check every 1–2 minutes until done. If the grill does not have an upper rack, place the pizzas on a couple of sheets of heavy-duty aluminum foil to prevent the bottom from burning while cheese melts.

Variation: For a thin crust, scoop out the middle of the cut bread pieces and fill with the toppings and cheese.

CAESAR SALAD

MAKES 2 TO 4 SERVINGS

Olive oil

2 to 4 hearts of romaine lettuce

10 to 12 small asparagus spears or 12 Brussels sprouts

3 tablespoons freshly grated Parmesan cheese

Homemade Croutons (page 34)

1 fresh lemon, sliced

Freshly ground black pepper, to taste

1 bottle Caesar salad dressing, of choice

Preheat grill to medium high and lightly oil grate.

Wash and pat dry the lettuce and cut in half lengthwise. If the heads of lettuce are loose and coming apart, you can tie them gently together with kitchen twine (moisten the twine with water after tying to ensure it does not burn). Brush cut sides with oil and grill until starting to caramelize, about 2 minutes. Remove from grill and set aside.

Wash and trim the woody ends of the asparagus, if using. Place in a shallow dish and toss with a small amount of oil to coat. Do the same for the Brussels sprouts, if using. Place asparagus or sprouts in a grill basket to prevent from falling through the grate, and cook until they start to soften and caramelize a bit, 5–10 minutes.

Place 2 halves of the grilled romaine hearts on each individual serving plate and evenly divide the asparagus or sprouts, cheese, croutons, and lemon slices over the top. Garnish with pepper and serve with dressing on the side.

Variation: Make this salad a meal and serve topped with Blackened Salmon (page 48) or BBQ Shrimp Scampi (page 47).

TUNA AND CHEESE MELTS

MAKES 2 SANDWICHES

Butter, to taste

4 slices bread, of choice

1 (6-ounce) can tuna, drained

2 to 4 tablespoons mayonnaise, or to taste

1 tablespoon sweet or dill pickle relish, or to taste

2 sandwich slices cheddar cheese

Tomato slices, optional

Preheat grill to medium high.

Lightly butter 1 side of each bread slice. Lay bread slices, buttered side down, on a plate.

In a small bowl, mix together the tuna, mayonnaise, and relish. Divide mixture in half and top 2 slices of bread with the tuna and the remaining slices of bread with cheese. Place filled bread slices on grill grate, buttered side down and cook for about 2 minutes, or until lightly toasted and cheese melts. Remove from grill and place a couple of tomato slices over tuna mixture on each sandwich. Top with remaining bread slices.

Variation: Try one of our family favorites and replace the tuna mixture with raspberry jam.

GRILLED BACON, LETTUCE, AND TOMATO SANDWICH

MAKES 2 SANDWICHES

1 to 2 tablespoons mayonnaise, or to taste

4 slices soft white bread

8 strips thick-cut peppered bacon, or of choice

1 large heirloom tomato, sliced

Salt and freshly ground pepper, to taste

2 to 4 leaves iceberg lettuce

Preheat grill to medium low.

Spread a thin layer of mayonnaise on 1 side of each bread slice. Lay the bread slices on the grill grate, mayonnaise side down, and grill for 45–60 seconds, or until golden brown.

Remove from the grill and spread a layer of mayonnaise on untoasted side of bread slices; set aside.

Place the bacon on a grill mat or sheet, or a couple layers of heavy-duty aluminum foil with the edges turned up, and place that on the grill, over indirect heat. Cook and turn bacon strips every 2–3 minutes to make sure they cook evenly, until cooked as desired. Remove from the grill and let drain on paper towels.

Assemble sandwiches by arranging 4 strips of bacon on 2 slices of bread over the mayonnaise. Place 1–2 slices of tomato over the bacon, season with salt and pepper, and add lettuce. Top with remaining bread slices.

QUESADILLA STACKS

MAKES 4 SERVINGS

8 (8-inch) flour tortillas

Vegetable oil or softened butter

4 cups grated Monterey Jack or cheddar cheese

Favorite toppings such as: sliced grilled chicken, green onions, fresh spinach leaves, black olives, green chiles, tomatoes, jalapeños, or avocado

Favorite salsa, for serving

Preheat grill to medium high.

Brush both sides of each tortilla with oil. Place tortillas on grill for 1–3 minutes, or until golden brown underneath. Flip tortillas over and sprinkle evenly with cheese. Layer your choice of toppings over 4 of the tortillas and continue to cook until cheese melts and the bottoms turn golden; remove from grill. Place 1 of the cheese only tortillas over the top of each filled tortilla, cheese side down. Serve with salsa on the side.

BBQ SHRIMP SCAMPI

MAKES 2 TO 3 SERVINGS

24 large shrimp, peeled and deveined

3 tablespoons butter

2 tablespoons minced fresh garlic, or to taste

2 tablespoons barbecue sauce, of choice

Chopped fresh parsley, for garnish, optional

Preheat grill to medium.

Place the shrimp, butter, garlic, and barbecue sauce in a large bowl; toss to coat. Arrange shrimp mixture on a sheet of heavy-duty aluminum foil. Cover the shrimp with a second sheet of foil and fold edges together to create a sealed packet.

Place foil packet on grill grate and cook for 4–5 minutes, or until shrimp start to turn pink and become slightly opaque and a little white. If the white is bright in color, the shrimp is probably overcooked. Garnish with parsley prior to serving.

Variation: Serve shrimp over Caesar Salad (page 37).

BLACKENED SALMON

MAKES 4 SERVINGS

BLACKENED RUB

4 teaspoons paprika

2 teaspoons salt

2 teaspoons pepper

2 teaspoons thyme

2 teaspoons onion powder

1 teaspoon garlic powder

1 teaspoon cayenne pepper

1 teaspoon dried oregano leaves

1 teaspoon dried basil

4 (3-ounce) salmon fillets

Combine rub ingredients together in a small bowl.

Coat the salmon fillets liberally and evenly with the rub, and store any leftovers in an airtight container in a cool, dry place. Place the salmon in the refrigerator for about 15 minutes.

Preheat grill to medium.

Lightly oil grate and place the salmon, skin side down, on grate, or use a grill basket. Close the lid and cook for 8–10 minutes depending on the thickness of the fillets, or until the flesh flakes easily with a fork. Turn once halfway through grilling. When finished cooking, remove from grill, and then remove skin prior to serving.

Variation: Serve blackened salmon fillets over Caesar Salad (page 37).

PERFECTLY GRILLED SALMON

MAKES 4 TO 6 SERVINGS

1 (2- to 3-pound) salmon fillet

½ cup mayonnaise

2 teaspoons lemon juice

Dried onions, to taste

Fresh or dried dill weed, to taste

Salt and freshly ground pepper, to taste

Preheat grill to medium.

Arrange salmon fillet, skin side down, on a sheet of heavy-duty aluminum foil large enough to completely wrap the fillet.

In a small bowl, combine the mayonnaise and lemon juice and spread over the salmon. Sprinkle dried onions and dill over top. Wrap the foil around the salmon and seal. Place packet on grill grate and cook for 15–20 minutes depending on the thickness of the fillet, or until the flesh flakes easily with a fork. Season with salt and pepper.

SEATTLE-STYLE SALMON

MAKES 4 TO 6 SERVINGS

1 (2- to 3-pound) salmon fillet

¼ to ½ cup chopped fresh scallops

1 large sweet onion, peeled and sliced

2 medium yellow squash, diced

1 medium zucchini, diced

1 pound small red or new potatoes, quartered

½ cup mayonnaise

2 teaspoons lemon juice

Salt and freshly ground pepper, to taste

Chopped fresh parsley, for garnish

Preheat grill to medium.

Arrange salmon fillet, skin side down, on a sheet of heavy-duty aluminum foil large enough to wrap the fillet, scallops, and vegetables. Arrange scallops, most of the onion slices, squash, zucchini, and potatoes around the salmon.

In a small bowl, combine the mayonnaise and lemon juice and spread over top of salmon. Place remaining onion slices over top of mayonnaise mixture. Wrap the foil around the salmon and vegetables and seal. Place on grill grate and cook for 15–20 minutes depending on the thickness of the fillet, or until the flesh flakes easily with a fork. Season with salt and pepper and garnish with parsley to serve.

PARMESAN HALIBUT

MAKES 2 TO 4 SERVINGS

1 medium sweet onion, sliced

2 tablespoons minced fresh garlic

¼ cup butter

2 teaspoons Dijon mustard

2 tablespoons lemon juice

¼ cup freshly grated Parmesan cheese

2 to 4 (⅓-pound) halibut fillets or steaks

Salt and freshly ground pepper, to taste

In a large frying pan, sauté onion and garlic in butter until tender. Add mustard, lemon juice, and cheese. Bring to a low simmer and cook for 3 minutes until cheese has fully melted, stirring to combine. Remove from heat and set aside.

Preheat grill to medium.

Place halibut on a sheet of heavy-duty aluminum foil and top with half of the onion mixture. Place on the grill grate, close the lid, and cook for 5–6 minutes per side, or until flesh flakes easily with a fork. Season with salt and pepper, and top with remaining onion mixture to serve.

LEMON-CILANTRO FISH FILLETS

MAKES 2 TO 4 SERVINGS

1 ½ pounds salmon, swordfish, or halibut fillets, about ¾–1 inch thick

1 teaspoon salt

¼ teaspoon pepper

¼ cup butter, melted

1 tablespoon lemon juice

2 teaspoons chopped fresh cilantro leaves

Lemon wedges, to serve

Preheat grill to medium.

Sprinkle fish evenly with salt and pepper and place on a sheet of heavy-duty aluminum foil large enough to completely wrap the fillets.

In a small bowl, mix together the butter, lemon juice, and cilantro and brush about ¼ of the mixture evenly over the fillets. Wrap the foil around the fish and seal. Place on grill grate and cook for 15–20 minutes, or until flesh flakes easily with a fork. Brush fillets 2–3 times during cooking with remaining butter mixture. Serve with lemon wedges.

JAZZED-UP BBQ STEAK

MAKES 2 TO 4 SERVINGS

2 to 4 sirloin steaks

1 recipe Jazzed-Up BBQ Sauce (page 118)

Preheat grill to high.

Place steaks on grill grate directly over the heat and sear for 1 minute on each side. Turn grill down to medium-low halfway through searing the second side. Move the steaks to area of indirect heat, the cooler side of the grill, and cook to desired doneness, turning the steaks once halfway through grilling process.

As steaks begin to reach optimal internal temperature, brush the tops with sauce and continue to cook for 60–90 seconds until sauce starts to glaze over. Turn the steaks and brush the other side with the sauce allowing same amount of time to glaze.

Remove from grill when the internal temperature of the steaks read approximately 5 degrees lower than the desired finished cooking temperature. Place on a serving plate and allow steaks to rest for about 5 minutes before serving.

CLASSIC RIB-EYE

MAKES 2 TO 4 SERVINGS

2 to 4 rib-eye steaks

1 recipe Steve's Famous Dry Rub
(page 125)

Smoker pouch (page 9)

Evenly rub the entire surface of each steak with Steve's Famous Dry Rub. If time allows, let the steaks rest at room temperature for 20–30 minutes before grilling.

Place a smoker pouch directly on the fire, under the grill grate, and turn grill to high heat until smoke begins to rise from the holes.

Place steaks on grill grate directly over the heat and sear for 1 minute on each side. Turn grill down to medium-low heat halfway through searing the second side. Move the steaks to area of indirect heat, the cooler side of the grill, and cook to desired doneness, turning the steaks once halfway through grilling process.

Remove from grill when the internal temperature of the steaks read approximately 5 degrees lower than the desired finished cooking temperature. Place on a serving plate and allow steaks to rest for about 5 minutes before serving.

TEMPTING T-BONE

MAKES 2 TO 4 SERVINGS

2 to 4 (1-inch-thick) T-bone steaks

1 to 2 tablespoons Steve's Famous Dry Rub (page 125), or to taste

1 to 2 tablespoons garlic salt, or to taste

Smoker pouch (page 9)

Evenly rub 1 side of each steak with the dry rub and the other side with garlic salt. Place steaks on a large plate and let sit at room temperature for 20–30 minutes before grilling, if possible.

Preheat grill to high.

Place the smoker pouch directly on the fire, under the grate, until smoke begins to rise from holes. Place steaks on grill grate directly over high heat for 30 seconds then turn and sear the other side for another 30 seconds, turning the heat down to medium halfway through searing the second side.

Move the steaks to the cooler side of the grill away from direct heat and cook to desired doneness, turning the steaks once about halfway through grilling. Remove from grill when the internal temperature on an instant-read thermometer reaches approximately 5 degrees lower than the desired finished temperature. Allow steaks to rest for about 5 minutes before serving.

HONEY-GARLIC BBQ SIRLOIN

MAKES 2 TO 4 SERVINGS

2 to 4 (1 ½-inch thick) sirloin steaks

1 recipe Honey-Garlic BBQ Sauce (page 121)

Preheat grill to high.

Place steaks on grill grate directly over high heat for 30 seconds, then turn and sear the other side for another 30 seconds, turning the heat down to medium halfway through searing the second side. Move the steaks to the cooler side of the grill away from direct heat and cook to desired doneness, turning the steaks once about halfway through grilling.

As the steaks begin to reach optimal temperature, brush the tops with sauce and continue to grill for about 1–1 ½ minutes until the sauce starts to glaze over. Turn the steaks over and brush with sauce, repeating the process.

Remove from grill when the internal temperature on an instant-read thermometer reaches approximately 5 degrees lower than the desired finished temperature. Allow steaks to rest for about 5 minutes before serving.

ISLAND-STYLE SIRLOIN STRIPS

MAKES 2 TO 4 SERVINGS

1 ½ pounds sirloin tip steak, cut into ½-inch-thick strips

1 ½ to 2 cups Island-Style Marinade (page 124)

Hot cooked rice, to serve

Place steak strips and marinade in a large covered bowl or ziplock bag, stir or shake to coat, and marinate in the refrigerator overnight.

When ready to cook, preheat grill to high.

Remove sirloin strips from marinade and lay across grill grate; cook for about 30 seconds on each side. Turn heat down to medium and continue cooking for 8–12 minutes, or until desired doneness, turning frequently. Serve over hot cooked rice.

Note: Boil the leftover marinade in a saucepan over high heat to make it safe to use as a warmed sauce drizzled over the rice.

GARLIC-RUBBED STEAKS

MAKES 2 TO 4 SERVINGS

2 to 4 (1–1 ½-inch-thick) steaks of choice, such as porterhouse, T-bone, rib-eye, New York strip, or top sirloin

1 tablespoon minced fresh garlic, or to taste

2 tablespoons food-safe rock salt

Montreal Steak Seasoning, to taste

Preheat grill to high.

Rub both sides of each steak evenly with minced garlic and rock salt. Place steaks on grill grate over direct heat and sear for 1 minute on each side. Turn heat down to medium and cook to desired doneness. Sprinkle both sides of each steak with seasoning, remove from grill, and allow to rest for about 5 minutes before serving.

TERIYAKI STEAK

MAKES 2 TO 4 SERVINGS

1 cup Kikkoman soy sauce

1 cup sugar

1 clove garlic, peeled and minced

1 tablespoon grated fresh ginger

3 green onions, sliced

2 to 4 steaks of choice (Cube steak is good with this recipe.)

Combine all ingredients except steaks in a medium saucepan and heat, stirring, until sugar dissolves. Pour into a deep dish to cool for a few minutes and add the steaks, turning to coat. Let steaks marinate for 1–2 hours, and no longer, before grilling. Remove steaks from refrigerator and marinade, place on a plate, and bring to room temperature.

Preheat grill to medium low.

Place steaks on grill grate and cook, turning every 4–5 minutes, until desired doneness. Remove steaks from grill and allow to rest for about 5 minutes before serving.

STEAK KEBABS WITH BITE

MAKES 2 TO 4 SERVINGS

2 to 4 country-style beef ribs or steaks, cut into 1-inch cubes

½ cup cider vinegar

1 cup vegetable oil

1 (1-ounce) envelope onion soup mix

2 teaspoons gourmet, teriyaki, or soy sauce

2 tablespoons minced fresh garlic

2 to 4 (10–12-inch) metal or bamboo* skewers

Place the meat in a medium bowl. In a separate bowl, mix together the vinegar, oil, soup mix, sauce, and garlic until well-combined. Pour over the meat and stir to coat. Marinate, covered, in refrigerator for 2–3 hours.

Preheat grill to medium high.

Thread marinated meat on skewers and lay across grill grate. Cook, turning every 5 minutes, until desired doneness.

Variation: Alternate whole mushrooms, bell pepper wedges, and onion wedges between steak pieces before grilling.

*Tip: If you use wooden or bamboo skewers, soak them in water for 30 minutes prior to use to prevent burning.

PERFECT PRIME RIB ROAST

MAKES 4 SERVINGS

1 (2-rib) prime rib roast, about 4 pounds

2 tablespoons olive oil

½ cup food-safe rock salt (It is okay to use table salt, just be a little more conservative.)

3 tablespoons garlic salt

Lightly coat the roast and ribs evenly with oil and rub in the rock salt and garlic salt.

Preheat grill to medium high.

Place the roast on the upper rack of grill, if possible, or in a cooler section of the grill out of direct heat. Position a large dripping pan under roast on lower rack or under the grill grate. Close lid and cook for 20–30 minutes per pound; turning roast every 45 minutes. Remove roast from grill when internal temperature gets within 5–10 degrees of desired level of doneness. Internal temperature of roast will rise another 10 degrees after you remove it from the grill. Shoot for an internal temperature of 130 degrees, if you like it rare, and 150 degrees if you like a medium cook. If you want it well-done, leave the roast on the grill until it reaches an internal temperature of 165 degrees.

Remove roast from grill to a serving platter, tent loosely with aluminum foil, and let it rest for 15 minutes.

BEST EVER BBQ BURGERS

MAKES 4 SERVINGS

1 pound lean ground beef

½ envelope dry onion soup mix

¼ cup quick cooking oats

1 egg, beaten

1 recipe Steve's Famous Dry Rub (page 125), to taste

4 slices cheese, of choice

4 hamburger buns

Toppings of choice

Preheat grill to medium.

In a large bowl, mix together the ground beef, soup mix, oats, and egg until well-combined. Form mixture into 4 patties; not too thick. The patties will shrink as they cook.

Place the patties on the grill grate, and sprinkle dry rub over the top. Flip and sprinkle other side. Close the lid and cook for 10–20 minutes, or until done to liking, turning once about halfway through. Remove from grill and top burgers with cheese slices. Serve in buns with favorite toppings.

SHREDDED BEEF BRISKET

MAKES 6 TO 8 SERVINGS

Smoker pouch (page 9)

1 (3- to 4-pound) beef brisket

1 recipe Mop Sauce (page 121)

2 cups favorite barbecue sauce, warmed

6 to 8 hamburger buns, toasted

Prepared coleslaw, to serve

Preheat grill to high.

Place smoker pouch directly on the fire under the grate and turn grill to high heat until smoke begins to rise from the holes. Immediately turn heat to medium-low and place brisket on upper rack of grill, if possible. If there is no upper rack, place brisket on a large piece of heavy-duty aluminum foil. Close lid and cook for 30 minutes before basting with Mop Sauce. Continue to cook, turning and basting the brisket every 30 minutes until internal temperature reaches 165–180 degrees, not to exceed 190 degrees. Remove from grill to a serving platter, tent loosely with aluminum foil, and let it rest for 10–15 minutes.

Using 2 forks, shred meat into fine pieces and mix in warmed barbecue sauce, or serve it on the side. Serve shredded meat on toasted buns topped with coleslaw.

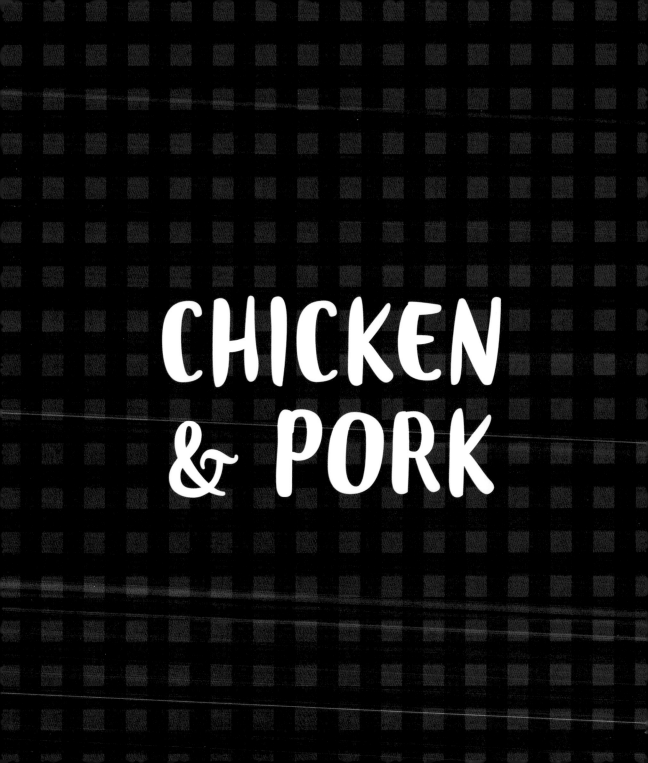

CHICKEN & PORK

STEVE'S FAMOUS DRY RUB CHICKEN ON A CAN

MAKES 4 TO 5 SERVINGS

Smoker pouch (page 9)

2 tablespoons butter, softened

1 recipe Steve's Famous Dry Rub (page 125)

1 whole chicken, rinsed and patted dry

1 (12-ounce) can regular soda such as a cola or Dr. Pepper

Place smoker pouch directly on the fire under the grill grate and turn grill to high heat until smoke begins to rise from the holes. Reduce heat to medium low.

Rub butter evenly over the chicken then rub the dry mix over the chicken to cover. Let sit at room temperature for at least 30 minutes before grilling.

Remove the upper grill rack and check to see if the whole chicken will fit standing up in the grill with the lid down. After you thoroughly wash and rinse the outside of the soda can, check to make sure the can will fit easily into the chicken's cavity. Remove the chicken and open the can of soda, placing the can on the grill rack or grate. Lower the chicken onto the can so that if fits into the cavity. Pull the legs forward to form a tripod to help give it some balance.

If your grill cooks hot, place a sheet of heavy-duty aluminum foil underneath the chicken. Close the lid and let it cook for 20 minutes per pound, or until an instant-read thermometer inserted into the thickest part of the thigh reaches 180 degrees (make sure not to touch bone).

Carefully transfer the chicken and can to a cutting board; both will be extremely hot. Let rest for 10–15 minutes, remove the can from the chicken and carve to serve.

ALABAMA-STYLE BBQ CHICKEN

MAKES 4 TO 6 SERVINGS

4 to 6 boneless, skinless chicken breasts

1 recipe Alabama White BBQ Sauce (page 120)

Preheat grill to low.

Place chicken over grill grate and cook, turning every 4–5 minutes, until juices run clear and internal temperature reaches 165 degrees.

During the last 5 minutes of cooking, coat the chicken with sauce, cook for about 2 minutes, and turn to baste the other side, cooking for 2–3 minutes.

Variation: Use a whole chicken that has been cut and quartered. Grill for 30–40 minutes, or until internal temperature reaches 165 degrees. Follow directions above for basting. This variation can be used for most of the chicken recipes in this chapter.

TANGY CHICKEN

MAKES 4 TO 6 SERVINGS

4 to 6 boneless, skinless chicken breasts

1 cup cider vinegar

½ cup vegetable oil

3 teaspoons minced fresh garlic

½ teaspoon poultry seasoning

1 tablespoon coarse salt

Place chicken in a large ziplock bag. In a small bowl, mix together the remaining ingredients, reserving some of the marinade to baste chicken with during the last few minutes of cooking time. Pour marinade over chicken and toss or shake to coat. Cover and place in refrigerator to marinate overnight.

Preheat grill to low.

Place chicken over grill grate and cook, turning every 4–5 minutes, until juices run clear and internal temperature reaches 165 degrees.

Once the chicken is done, baste with reserved marinade, and leave on grill long enough for the marinade to glaze over a bit.

SMOKED HONEY-GARLIC CHICKEN

MAKES 4 TO 6 SERVINGS

4 to 6 boneless, skinless chicken breasts

1 recipe Honey-Garlic BBQ Sauce (page 121)

Smoker pouch (page 9)

Cinnamon, to serve

Place chicken in a large ziplock bag. Add sauce, toss or shake to coat, and place in refrigerator to marinate for at least 30 minutes, or overnight, before grilling.

When ready to grill the chicken, place smoker pouch directly on the fire under the grill grate and turn the grill to high heat until smoke begins to rise from holes. Reduce heat to low, place chicken over grill grate, and cook, turning every 4–5 minutes, until juices run clear and internal temperature reaches 165 degrees.

Dust chicken with cinnamon when ready to serve.

ORANGE-SESAME CHICKEN

MAKES 8 SERVINGS

8 boneless, skinless chicken thighs

½ cup orange juice

1 tablespoon lemon juice

1 tablespoon vinegar

2 teaspoons yellow mustard

2 tablespoons toasted sesame oil

Salt and freshly ground pepper, to taste

Place chicken in a shallow baking dish or a large ziplock bag. In a small bowl, mix together the orange juice, lemon juice, vinegar, and mustard. Whisk the oil in slowly. Pour marinade over chicken, reserving some of the marinade to baste chicken with during the last few minutes of cooking time. Pour over chicken and toss or shake to coat. Cover and place in refrigerator to marinate for 2 hours.

Preheat grill to medium low.

Place chicken over grill grate and cook, turning every 4–5 minutes, until juices run clear and internal temperature reaches 165 degrees.

Once the chicken is done, baste with reserved marinade, and leave on grill long enough for the marinade to glaze over a bit.

SUCCULENT CHICKEN

MAKES 3 TO 5 SERVINGS

8 to 10 boneless, skinless chicken thighs

1 cup soy sauce

1 cup water

2 cups brown sugar

1 tablespoon minced fresh garlic

1 tablespoon minced fresh ginger

2 lemon or orange slices

2 tablespoons minced fresh green onion

Place chicken in a large ziplock bag. In a medium bowl, mix together the remaining ingredients and pour over the chicken; toss or shake to coat. Cover and place in refrigerator to marinate overnight.

Preheat grill to low.

Place chicken over grill grate and cook, turning every 4–5 minutes, until juices run clear and internal temperature reaches 165 degrees.

GRANDMA'S COLA CHICKEN

MAKES 3 TO 5 SERVINGS

1 cup flour

1 ½ pounds chicken tenders

1 (14-ounce) bottle ketchup

½ (12-ounce) can regular cola

Preheat grill to low heat.

Place flour in a medium bowl. Working in batches, dredge chicken tenders through flour to coat.

In a separate bowl, stir together the ketchup and cola until thoroughly combined; set aside.

Place chicken over grill grate and cook, turning every 4–5 minutes, until juices run clear and internal temperature reaches 165 degrees.

Baste chicken with cola sauce during the last 5 minutes of grilling, turning every 1–2 minutes.

ISLAND-GRILLED TERIYAKI CHICKEN

MAKES 2 TO 5 SERVINGS

8 to 10 boneless, skinless chicken thighs

2 cups Yoshida's Gourmet Sauce or teriyaki sauce, of choice

1 tablespoon minced fresh garlic, or to taste

½ medium sweet onion, peeled and finely chopped

2 green onions or scallions, chopped

Place chicken in a large ziplock bag. In a medium bowl, mix together the remaining ingredients, reserving some of the marinade to baste chicken with during the last few minutes of cooking time. Pour over chicken and toss or shake to coat. Cover and place in refrigerator to marinate overnight.

Preheat grill to low.

Place chicken over grill grate and cook, turning every 4–5 minutes, until juices run clear and internal temperature reaches 165 degrees.

Once the chicken is done, baste with reserved marinade and leave on grill long enough for the marinade to glaze over.

MONDAY-NIGHT-SPECIAL BUFFALO WINGS

MAKES 2 TO 4 SERVINGS

1 cup spicy barbecue sauce, of choice

2 to 3 tablespoons Tabasco Pepper Sauce, or to taste

2 tablespoons brown sugar

1 tablespoon vinegar

¼ teaspoon freshly ground pepper

2 dozen chicken wings or wing drummies

Celery sticks, for serving

Blue cheese salad dressing, for serving

In a small saucepan, combine all ingredients except wings and bring to a boil. Remove from heat, pour into a large bowl, and let cool for 15 minutes. Add chicken wings to marinade and chill 2 hours or more.

Preheat grill to medium low.

Place wings over grill grate and cook for 10–15 minutes, or until juices run clear and internal temperature reaches 165 degrees, turning every 4–5 minutes.

Serve with celery and salad dressing on the side.

JAZZY BBQ TURKEY LEGS

MAKES 2 TO 4 SERVINGS

2 to 4 turkey legs

1 recipe Jazzed-Up BBQ Sauce
(page 118)

Preheat grill to medium high.

Place turkey legs over grill grate and cook for 30–45 minutes, or until juices run clear and internal temperature reaches 165 degrees, turning occasionally.

During the last 5 minutes of cooking, baste turkey with sauce, turning to coat completely. Serve hot with any extra sauce, heated, on the side.

JAZZED-UP CHICKEN

MAKES 4 TO 6 SERVINGS

4 to 6 boneless, skinless chicken breasts

1 recipe Jazzed-Up BBQ Sauce (page 118)

2 red bell peppers, sliced

1 yellow onion, peeled and sliced

1 tablespoon butter

Preheat grill to medium low.

Place chicken over grill grate and cook, turning every 4–5 minutes, until juices run clear and internal temperature reaches 165 degrees.

Baste chicken with sauce during last 5 minutes of cooking, turning every 1–2 minutes. Remove chicken from grill and let rest for 2–3 minutes before serving.

While chicken is cooking, place the peppers, onion, and butter in a medium frying pan, and sauté until tender. Serve over chicken.

PERFECT RUBBED RIBS

MAKES 2 TO 4 SERVINGS

1 to 2 (3- to 4-pound) racks pork ribs or pork spareribs*

1 recipe Steve's Brown Sugar Rub (page 124)

Peel film off back of ribs by hand, or carefully using a knife. Rub the ribs thoroughly with dry rub and let rest for about 1 hour before grilling.

Preheat grill to medium low.

Place ribs on grill grate out of direct heat, cover with lid, and cook slowly for 30–40 minutes, or until internal temperature reaches 190–200 degrees, turning occasionally.

*Tip: To enhance and give ribs a more robust flavor, soak them in Pork and Poultry Brine (page 123) for 1–2 hours before grilling.

Variation: Ask your grocer's meat department to rip (or cut) ribs lengthwise to create bite-size riblets.

RASPBERRY PORK LOIN

MAKES 4 TO 6 SERVINGS

2 (1-pound) pork tenderloins

1 recipe Pork and Poultry Brine (page 123) or more if needed

1 recipe Steve's Brown Sugar Rub (page 124), to taste

RASPBERRY BBQ SAUCE

1 cup fresh raspberry jam with seeds

1 (18-ounce) bottle barbecue sauce, of choice

Finely diced onion, brown sugar, mustard, or horseradish, to taste, optional

Place tenderloins in a deep dish and cover with brine. Marinate for 60 minutes per pound before grilling. Remove from brine, rinse well, and pat dry. Evenly coat tenderloins with rub.

Preheat grill to medium.

Place tenderloins on grill grate and cook for 30–40 minutes per side, or until internal temperature reaches 145–165 degrees. As you reach desired temperature, reduce heat to low. Mix together the ingredients for the Raspberry BBQ Sauce and baste tenderloins during the last 3–4 minutes of cooking time until glazed. Turn and baste the other side of each loin, allowing sauce to glaze over, about 1 minute.

SWEET-AS-HONEY PORK LOIN

MAKES 4 TO 6 SERVINGS

2 (1-pound) pork tenderloins

1 recipe Pork and Poultry Brine
(page 123) or more if needed

1 recipe Steve's Brown Sugar Rub
(page 124)

Honey, to taste

Place tenderloins in a deep dish and cover with brine. Marinate for 60 minutes per pound before grilling. Remove from brine, rinse well, and pat dry. Evenly coat tenderloins with rub.

Preheat grill to medium.

Place tenderloins on grill grate and cook for 30–40 minutes per side, or until internal temperature reaches 145–165 degrees. As you reach desired temperature, drizzle honey evenly over the tenderloins during the last 3–4 minutes of cooking time until glazed. Turn and drizzle honey on the other side of each loin, allowing sauce to glaze over, about 1 minute.

BIG RED'S CHOPS

MAKES 2 TO 4 SERVINGS

2 to 4 center-cut pork chops or
steaks, 1 inch thick

1 recipe Big Red's Spicy Dry Rub
(page 125)

1 cup barbecue sauce, of choice

Rub chops thoroughly with dry rub and let sit 20–40 minutes before grilling.

Preheat grill to medium.

Place chops on grill grate out of direct heat. Cook for 10–12 minutes per side, or until internal temperature reaches 145–160 degrees, depending on taste. Serve with barbecue sauce on the side.

KICKIN' MUSTARD RIBS

MAKES 2 TO 4 SERVINGS

1 to 2 (3- to 4- pound) racks pork ribs or pork spareribs*

1 cup mustard

¼ cup honey

2 tablespoons paprika

¼ cup brown sugar

1 tablespoon garlic powder

1 ½ to 2 tablespoons cider vinegar

1 to 2 tablespoons chili powder

Preheat grill to medium low.

Peel film off back of ribs by hand, or carefully using a knife.

In a small bowl, mix together the mustard, honey, paprika, brown sugar, garlic powder, vinegar, and chili powder. Spread sauce evenly over the ribs.

Place ribs on grill grate out of direct heat, cover with lid, and cook slowly for 30–40 minutes, or until internal temperature reaches 190–200 degrees, turning occasionally.

*Tip: To enhance and give ribs a more robust flavor, soak them in Pork and Poultry Brine (page 123) for 1–2 hours before grilling.

Variation: Ask your grocer's meat department to rip (or cut) ribs lengthwise to create bite-size riblets.

CRAZY-GOOD BRINED PORK CHOPS

MAKES 2 TO 4 SERVINGS

2 to 4 (1-inch thick) center-cut pork chops or steaks

1 recipe Pork and Poultry Brine (page 123)

1 recipe Steve's Brown Sugar Rub (page 124)

Place chops in brine and marinate in refrigerator for 45–60 minutes prior to grilling. Make sure there is enough brine to completely cover the chops.

Remove chops from brine, rinse, and pat dry.

Preheat grill to medium.

Season both sides of each chop with the dry rub, and then place in coolest part of the grill, out of direct heat. Close lid and cook for 10–12 minutes per side, or until internal temperature reaches 145–160 degrees, depending on your taste. Remove chops from grill and let rest for about 10 minutes before serving.

Variation: Brush Raspberry BBQ Sauce (page 93) over chops during the last 2–3 minutes of grilling time just until glazed. Flip chops over and apply sauce to the other side and allow to glaze over for about 1 minute.

DRY RUB PULLED PORK

MAKES 3 TO 5 SERVINGS

Smoker pouch (page 9)

1 (3- to 5- pound) pork shoulder roast

1 recipe Steve's Brown Sugar Rub (page 124)

2 cups barbecue sauce, of choice, heated

Place smoker pouch directly on the fire under the grate and turn to high heat until smoke begins to rise from holes. Reduce heat to medium low.

Rub roast thoroughly with dry rub. Place the roast on upper grill rack, or over a sheet of heavy-duty aluminum foil if the grill only has 1 level. Close the lid and cook for 15–20 minutes per pound, or until internal temperature reaches 195 degrees, turning roast every 15–20 minutes. Remove from grill to a shallow serving dish and allow to rest for 10–15 minutes.

Using 2 forks, tear the roast into fine shreds. Add barbecue sauce to shredded meat, or serve separately on the side.

Variation: For a spicier version, use Big Red's Spicy Dry Rub (page 125).

SMOKED HONEY-GARLIC BBQ PORK

MAKES 2 TO 4 SERVINGS

1 recipe Honey-Garlic BBQ Sauce (page 121)

¼ teaspoon curry powder

2 to 4 (1-inch-thick) center-cut pork chops or steaks

Smoker pouch (page 9)

In a small bowl, combine Honey-Garlic BBQ Sauce with curry; reserve some of the sauce for basting.

Place chops in a shallow dish and cover with the marinade. Let rest at room temperature for 30–60 minutes before grilling.

Place smoker pouch directly on the fire under the grate and turn grill to high heat until smoke begins to rise from holes. Immediately turn heat down to medium low.

Place chops on grill grate and cook for 15–20 minutes on the upper rack for best smoking results. Chops are done when the internal temperature reaches 145–160 degrees. During the last 5 minutes of cooking, baste chops with reserved sauce, turning every 2 minutes. Remove from grill and allow to rest for 2–3 minutes before serving.

SPICY RUBBED PORK ROAST

MAKES 4 TO 6 SERVINGS

Smoker pouch (page 9)

1 (3- to 5-pound) pork shoulder roast

1 recipe Big Red's Spicy Dry Rub (page 125)

2 cups barbecue sauce, of choice, warmed

4 to 6 buns or rolls, of choice

Place smoker pouch directly on the fire under the grate and turn to high heat until smoke begins to rise from holes. Immediately turn heat down to medium low.

Rub roast thoroughly with dry rub and place on upper grill rack, or use a piece of heavy-duty aluminum foil underneath the roast if grill only has 1 level. Grill for 15–20 minutes per pound, or until the internal temperature reaches 165–180 degrees. Turn roast every 15–20 minutes, until done. Remove from grill and allow to rest for 10–15 minutes.

Using 2 forks, tear meat into fine shreds. Mix shredded meat with barbecue sauce and serve on buns.

BOY'S-NIGHT-OUT ORANGE RIBS

MAKES 2 TO 4 SERVINGS

1 rack pork ribs or pork spare ribs*

1 recipe Steve's Brown Sugar Rub (page 124), to taste

½ cup salsa, of choice

¼ cup chili sauce

3 tablespoons orange marmalade

Peel film off back of ribs by hand, or carefully using a knife. Rub the ribs thoroughly with dry rub and let rest for about 1 hour before grilling.

In a small bowl, combine salsa, chili sauce, and marmalade together.

Preheat grill to medium low.

Place ribs on grill grate out of direct heat, cover with lid, and cook slowly for 30–40 minutes, or until internal temperature reaches 190–200 degrees, turning occasionally. Baste with sauce during the last 5 minutes of grilling.

*Tip: To enhance and give ribs a more robust flavor, soak them in Pork and Poultry Brine (page 123) for 1–2 hours before grilling.

Variation: Ask your grocer's meat department to rip (or cut) ribs lengthwise to create bite-size riblets.

JUST
DESSERTS

S'MORE CHOCOLATE CHIP COOKIES

MAKES 6 SERVINGS

3 (1.55-ounce) Hershey's Milk Chocolate bars

12 homemade chocolate chip cookies

6 large marshmallows

Preheat grill to medium high.

Break each chocolate bar into 2 equal halves. Place each of the halves between the flat sides of 2 cookies and set aside.

Place 1 marshmallow on a skewer or marshmallow stick and hold over the hot part of the grill, turning constantly to achieve an even, light golden brown color, or until the marshmallow begins to melt, about 4–5 minutes.

Remove the marshmallow from the skewer by placing it between 2 cookies over the piece of chocolate and gently pulling the skewer through. Repeat with remaining ingredients.

FRUIT DELIGHT

MAKES 1 TO 2 SERVINGS PER PIECE OF UNCUT FRUIT

Choice of fresh fruit, such as Red or Golden Delicious apples, pears, peaches, or pineapple

1 cup brown sugar

1 tablespoon ground cinnamon

1 to 2 fresh sprigs thyme, optional

Preheat grill to medium high.

Wash, core, and cut fruit into uniform ½-inch-thick slices or wedges.

Mix brown sugar and cinnamon in a large bowl or ziplock bag. Add the fruit slices in batches and toss or shake to coat completely.

Lay coated fruit across a lightly oiled grill grate or in a grill basket and cook for 2–3 minutes per side, or until heated through and grill marks appear. Garnish sparingly with thyme.

BANANA BOATS

MAKES 4 SERVINGS

4 ripe firm bananas

½ cup chocolate chips

½ cup miniature marshmallows

Preheat grill to medium high.

Peel 1 section of each banana from top to bottom, remove, and discard that section of peel. Following the outline of the remaining peel on the banana, cut out and remove a thin wedge of banana the same shape as the exposed fruit.

Fill the space in the top of each banana with an even mixture of chocolate chips and marshmallows. Place bananas on grill out of direct heat, close the lid and let cook for approximately 2–3 minutes, or until the chocolate chips start to melt and marshmallows begin to turn golden.

GRILLED CANTALOUPE

MAKES 4 SERVINGS

1 large ripe cantaloupe

½ cup sugar

4 (10- to 12-inch) metal or bamboo* skewers

Vanilla ice cream, to serve, optional

Preheat grill to medium.

Wash and scrub cantaloupe before cutting; pat dry with paper towels. Cut off the top and bottom of the melon and then carefully remove strips of rind by cutting from top to bottom following the curves of the melon. Cut away any remaining green portions. Cut the melon in half and gently scrape out the seeds and pulp with a spoon; discard. Cut each half into even wedges and each wedge into chunks.

Place melon chunks in a large bowl and sprinkle sugar over top; toss to coat. Thread chunks on skewers and lay across lightly oiled grill grate. Cook for 3–4 minutes, or until warmed and grill marks start to appear, turning once during cooking time. Serve warm over ice cream, if desired.

*Tip: If you use wooden or bamboo skewers, soak them in water for 30 minutes prior to using so they don't burn.

CINNAMON ROLLED SNAIL SNACKS

MAKES 2 TO 4 SERVINGS

¼ cup sugar

1 tablespoon ground cinnamon

4 slices white bread

Butter, softened

Preheat grill to medium.

In a small bowl, mix together the sugar and cinnamon. Trim the crusts from each slice of bread; discard crusts.

Flatten the bread slices slightly with a rolling pin and then spread a thin coat of butter over 1 side of each piece of bread. Sprinkle the cinnamon and sugar mixture evenly over the buttered side. Roll the bread with the filling on the inside, into a tight roll; secure with toothpicks that have been soaked in water.

Lay bread rolls across lightly oiled grill grate and cook for 2–3 minutes, turning every minute until lightly toasted. Remove from grill and cut into 1-inch pieces to serve.

SAUCES & RUBS

JAZZED-UP BBQ SAUCE

MAKES ABOUT 2 $\frac{1}{2}$ CUPS

1 (18-ounce) bottle barbecue sauce, of choice

SUGGESTED MIX-INS

$\frac{1}{2}$ can regular cola

1 tablespoon minced garlic

2 tablespoons brown sugar (great with pork)

1 tablespoon honey (great with pork)

$\frac{1}{2}$ sweet onion, finely diced

1 teaspoon liquid smoke

1 tablespoon Worcestershire sauce

1 tablespoon favorite salsa

$\frac{1}{4}$ teaspoon cayenne pepper

$\frac{1}{2}$ teaspoon horseradish

Add barbecue sauce to a medium bowl and mix in any or all of the listed ingredients to create your own signature sauce.

SAUCING

Barbecue sauce is not a marinade. Marinating is soaking tough cuts of meat in sauce designed not only to add flavor, but to help break down some of the tough parts of the meat and tenderize it.

Only apply barbecue sauce to the meat after it is done cooking. Putting the sauce on while the meat is cooking will burn the sauce.

When the meat is done cooking, turn the grill down to low and leave the lid open for about 1 minute to cool the air in the grill. Then apply a liberal coat of barbecue sauce. You are not trying to cook the sauce. You just warm it and get it to glaze over and bind to the outside of the meat.

SWEET-AND-SAUCY BBQ SAUCE

MAKES 1 $\frac{1}{2}$ CUPS

1 cup ketchup

½ cup brown sugar

¼ cup mustard

½ tablespoon Worcestershire sauce

1 tablespoon vinegar

½ teaspoon ground ginger

Mix all ingredients together in a small bowl. Refrigerate any unused sauce in a covered container.

ALABAMA WHITE BBQ SAUCE

MAKES 1 $\frac{1}{2}$ CUPS

1 cup mayonnaise

½ cup vinegar (preferably cider)

1 tablespoon lemon juice

¼ to ½ teaspoon horseradish or cayenne pepper

1 teaspoon minced fresh garlic

Salt and freshly ground pepper, to taste

Mix all ingredients together in a small bowl, cover, and place in the refrigerator for at least 8 hours before using. Refrigerate any unused sauce in a covered container.

Note: This sauce is quite thin so it works best to slowly drizzle the sauce over the meat with a large spoon. After you drizzle the sauce on the meat, make sure it has time to glaze over, or it will taste rather bitter. Because of this, do not add sauce after you have taken the meat off of the grill.

MOP SAUCE

MAKES ABOUT 2 CUPS

1 cup cider vinegar
2 tablespoons salt
1 tablespoon brown sugar
1 teaspoon minced fresh garlic
1 tablespoon dried chopped onion
1 teaspoon horseradish or cayenne pepper
1/2 cup regular cola or root beer

Mix all ingredients together in a medium bowl. Refrigerate any unused sauce in a covered container.

Tips: Marinating meat in sauce for about 30 minutes per pound before grilling gives meat a more robust flavor and tenderizes it by breaking down the tough collagen fibers.

Basting meat with the Mop Sauce every 20–30 minutes while cooking will help tenderize it.

Low sugar levels reduce the likelihood of burning this sauce. If you struggle with burning the sauce on the outside of the meat then reduce the sugar or eliminate it.

HONEY-GARLIC BBQ SAUCE

MAKES 2 1/2 CUPS

1 (18-ounce) bottle barbecue sauce, of choice
1/2 (12-ounce) can regular cola
1/4 cup honey
1 to 2 tablespoons minced fresh garlic

Mix all ingredients together in a small bowl until well-combined. Refrigerate any unused sauce in a covered container.

SAUCE FROM SCRATCH

MAKES 2 $\frac{1}{4}$ CUPS

$\frac{1}{2}$ envelope dry onion soup mix

$\frac{1}{2}$ cup brown sugar

2 cups ketchup

$\frac{1}{2}$ teaspoon Worcestershire sauce

1 teaspoon minced fresh garlic

Mix all ingredients together in a small bowl. Marinate meat in sauce at least 30 minutes before grilling to give meat a more robust flavor.

FANTASTIC SAUCE

MAKES ABOUT 2 $\frac{1}{4}$ CUPS

$\frac{1}{2}$ (18-ounce) bottle hickory smoke barbecue sauce or steak sauce

1 cup Dr. Pepper

$\frac{1}{2}$ cup ketchup

2 tablespoons lemon juice

1 tablespoon cider vinegar

Mix all ingredients together in a small bowl, cover, and place in the refrigerator for at least 8 hours before using. Refrigerate any unused sauce in a covered container. This also makes a great dipping sauce, so reserve a small portion and serve on the side.

HAWAIIAN GINGER MARINADE

MAKES 1 $\frac{1}{4}$ CUPS

$\frac{1}{4}$ cup sugar

$\frac{1}{4}$ cup soy sauce

$\frac{1}{4}$ cup vegetable oil

$\frac{1}{4}$ cup water

2 tablespoons molasses

2 teaspoons minced fresh garlic

1 teaspoon ground ginger

1 teaspoon dry mustard

1 teaspoon salt

Combine all ingredients together in a blender until smooth. Pour into a covered container and store in refrigerator until ready to use. Shake before using.

PORK AND POULTRY BRINE

MAKES 1 CUP

1 cup water

1 tablespoon kosher salt

1 tablespoon sugar

Mix all ingredients together in a small bowl. If brining a lot of meat, make enough to cover completely. Let meat soak in brine for approximately 1 hour per pound.

ISLAND-STYLE MARINADE

MAKES 2 $\frac{1}{2}$ CUPS

1 cup soy sauce

1 cup water

2 cups brown sugar

1 tablespoon minced fresh garlic

1 tablespoon minced fresh ginger

2 fresh lemon or orange slices

2 tablespoons minced green onion

Mix all ingredients together in a small bowl. Marinate meat in sauce at least 30 minutes before grilling to give meat a more robust flavor.

STEVE'S BROWN SUGAR RUB

MAKES ABOUT 1 $\frac{1}{2}$ CUPS

$\frac{1}{2}$ cup sugar

$\frac{1}{2}$ cup brown sugar

$\frac{1}{4}$ cup coarse salt

2 tablespoons freshly ground black pepper

2 tablespoons dried chopped onion

1 tablespoon paprika

1 tablespoon garlic salt

Mix all ingredients together in a small bowl. Rub over your favorite cut of meat about 60 minutes prior to grilling.

Store any unused rub in an air-tight container.

STEVE'S FAMOUS DRY RUB

MAKES $^1/_2$ CUP

1 tablespoon coarse salt

1 tablespoon sugar

1 tablespoon celery salt

1 tablespoon brown sugar

1 tablespoon garlic salt

1 tablespoon freshly ground
black pepper

2 tablespoons paprika

Mix all ingredients together in a small bowl. Store any unused rub in an air-tight container.

BIG RED'S SPICY DRY RUB

MAKES 2 $^1/_4$ CUPS

½ cup freshly ground black
pepper

½ cup ground cayenne pepper

1 cup dark brown sugar

3 tablespoons salt

1 teaspoon garlic powder

Mix all ingredients together in a small bowl. Rub over your favorite cut of meat about 60 minutes prior to grilling.

Store any unused rub in an air-tight container.

INDEX

METRIC CONVERSION CHART

VOLUME MEASUREMENTS		WEIGHT MEASUREMENTS		TEMPERATURE CONVERSION	
U.S.	METRIC	U.S.	METRIC	FAHRENHEIT	CELSIUS
1 teaspoon	5 ml	½ ounce	15 g	250	120
1 tablespoon	15 ml	1 ounce	30 g	300	150
¼ cup	60 ml	3 ounces	80 g	325	160
⅓ cup	80 ml	4 ounces	115 g	350	175
½ cup	125 ml	8 ounces	225 g	375	190
⅔ cup	160 ml	12 ounces	340 g	400	200
¾ cup	180 ml	1 pound	450 g	425	220
1 cup	250 ml	2 ¼ pounds	1 kg	450	230